Insects and Sustainability: The

Among the Tāngkhul-Nag

CW00422189

TABLE OF CONTENTS

Insects and Sustainability: The Practice of Entomophagy Among the Tāngkhul-Naga Tribe of Manipur

CHAPTER I: INTRODUCTION

Entomophagy, the consumption of insects as food has been in practice in India for many years by various tribes, and this continues to be widely practiced among the Tāngkhul Naga Tribe (Tāngkhuls) living in the North-Eastern parts of India. Found mainly in the mountainous and rural region of Ukhrul District in the modern Indian State of Manipur, the Tāngkhuls are avid insect eaters. There is no denying the fact that living in difficult mountainous terrain makes the Tāngkhuls to suffer from scarcity of food, but lack of innovation and development also allows them to suffer from less food-option, making

Insects and Sustainability: The Practice of Entomophagy Among the Tāngkhul-Naga Tribe of Manipur

them to resort to consuming and eating any edible food they can find. Consumption of insects however indicates that food scarcity is easily met and that balance diet is observed, since insects are dietary supplement of meat and contains rich amount of protein, vitamins, and minerals. This fact is supported by the United Nations' Food and Agriculture Organization report that shows that eating insects can help boost nutrition, and help people to cope with food and feed issue (FAO 2013).

It is reported that there are more than 2 billion people worldwide (Spiegel 2015), who supplements their diets with insects. These people mostly reside in the

Insects and Sustainability: The Practice of Entomophagy Among the Tāngkhul-Naga Tribe of Manipur

Eastern hemisphere, since consuming insects still remains a barrier in Western countries. Food preferences remain highly local, and food habits are often associated with communities, society, race, or country, and for those in the West, insects at present are considered as *eww* factor (Goldman 1992). However, influence in food consumption will allow it to become a cultural norm in the future. People who do not consume insects often associate insects with filth, death, and decay, depending on what they feed on. Language surrounding food insects like "worms" also comes to be associated with wriggly living things that are unfit for consumption (Goldman 1992). People

Insects and Sustainability: The Practice of Entomophagy Among the Tāngkhul-Naga Tribe of Manipur

also see insects as equivalent of wood or paper, and dangerous or poisonous to consume by non-eaters. Others simply associates insects with disgust and considered them as barbarous to eat. Psychologically, it therefore becomes difficult for people to ingest insects.

Human has never shown aversion to entomophagy. They started with insectivorous diet, and evolved towards consuming fruits and vegetables; eventually practicing meat eating through hunting; and finally undergoing food satiety through cultivation (Pager 1973; Ramos-Elorduy 2009; Bodenheimer 2013). From academic stand, the practice of ethical

Insects and Sustainability: The Practice of Entomophagy Among the Tāngkhul-Naga Tribe of Manipur

entomophagy was emphasized since 1885 by Holt (1885) in his, *Why Not Eat Insects?*, followed by eminent work of Defoliart (1999) on how ingesting insects as food gives nutritional, economic, and ecological benefits to the people. Recent work of van Huis et al. (2010) and Tan et al. (2015) shows evolutionary pattern, where the environmental advantages and nutritional benefits are making people to take interest in entomophagy that goes beyond primal culture of indigenous people, but becomes a part of organized farming and progressive insect-based market products and systems. Environmentally, their studies show that livestock

Insects and Sustainability: The Practice of Entomophagy Among the Tāngkhul-Naga Tribe of Manipur

produces high amount of ammonia (NH3) that contributes towards Greenhouse Gas (GHG) emissions, as well as nitrification and acidification of soil; while rearing edible insects show relatively lower amounts of GHG emissions and NH3, as compared to conventional livestock (van Huis et al. 2010; Tan et al. 2015). Nutritionally, eating insects contributes higher content of protein, vitamins, and minerals to human body as compared to animals (Tan et al. 2015; van Huis et al. 2010). From the stand of sustainability, the Food and Agriculture Organization of the United Nations has been bringing out the need to substitute meat products with insects (FAO 2013). Scarcity of

Insects and Sustainability: The Practice of Entomophagy Among the Tāngkhul-Naga Tribe of Manipur

meat and food and the question of sustainability are likely to lead human society towards entomophagy.

Insects and Sustainability: The Practice of Entomophagy Among the Tāngkhul-Naga Tribe of Manipur

Insects and Sustainability: The Practice of Entomophagy Among the Tāngkhul-Naga Tribe of Manipur

CHAPTER II: SUSTAINABILITY AND ENTOMOPHAGOUS PRACTICE OF THE TĀNGKHUL-NAGA TRIBE

In India, majority of the poor people live in rural areas, where scarcity of food constitutes one of the main problems owing to poor food supply and distribution systems, and high prices of food, conditioned by lack of transport in the difficult geographical terrain. Against such challenges, practicing entomophagy helps in solving food crisis, since edible insects are not only a natural renewable food resource, but it is also nutritious, healthy, economical, and ecological in nature. Many of the tribes living in North-Eastern states of India also practices entomophagy, and

Insects and Sustainability: The Practice of Entomophagy Among the Tāngkhul-Naga Tribe of Manipur

among these tribes, the Tāngkhuls come out as prominent insect consumer. Many of the insects consumed by this tribe are found in the field, wetlands, river, and deep forests. Insects are not easy to capture, but there are simple methods like using small fishing nets or trap lights to capture them. On the one hand, organized farming in the form of sericulture and its products – mulberry silkworm does not involve hunting in wild forests or fields, but are harvested from its farm; on the other hand, organized farming of insects are available only in the form of sericulture, heliculture, and bee-keeping within this tribe. If facilities for rearing and harvesting of insects are available, high production and distribution can be taken up on large scale to solve food issues in the region, thereby ushering better livelihood. However, such organized farming practices still remains unexploited by the tribe owing to many developmental, financial, technological, and managerial challenges.

3.1. SILKWORM AND ITS LARVAE

Among the Tāngkhul-Naga Tribe, one of the most favourable stages of insect consumption is when they are in pupae or larvae stages. This goes for popular edible insects like mulberry silkworm, bee larvae, and wood-boring larvae.

Insects and Sustainability: The Practice of Entomophagy Among the Tāngkhul-Naga Tribe of Manipur

Silkworm Larvae (*Bombyx mori*)

Phot credit: Kachuiwung Ronra Shimray

Sericulture of the mulberry silkworm or *Bombyx mori* [*Kahāra̱rong Kulom*] is the largest organized and recognized farming of insects at present, which nevertheless is the threshold towards insect rearing and cultivation among the Tāngkhuls. Heliculture and bee-keeping are also practiced on recognized scale, although they still lack organized and structured farming. Sericulture involves using simple technologies, making the farming to become organized in nature. The farming proves advantageous for economically backward section of the society, since it gives self-employment to the people (Aruga 1994; Narasaiah 2003). Silkworm works as food products after its silk has been extracted, thereby forming a by-product for the people.

3.2. ASIAN HORNET AND ITS LARVAE

Bees and bees' larvae [*Khuī*] are also widely consumed by the Tāngkhuls, and although bee-

Insects and Sustainability: The Practice of Entomophagy Among the Tāngkhul-Naga Tribe of Manipur

farming are not practiced on a wide organized scale like sericulture, many Apiarists engaged in keeping bees. In fact, bee-keeping is the oldest insect rearing traditional industry among the tribe. Among the different species of bees consumed by this tribe, Asian Hornet or *Vespa mandarinia* [*Khuirei*] remains as the biggest, and the one that is popularly and widely consumed by the Tāngkhuls.

Insects and Sustainability: The Practice of Entomophagy Among the Tāngkhul-Naga Tribe of Manipur

Larvae of Asian Hornet (*Vespa madarinia*)

Besides bee-keeping, bees and bees' larvae are also collected from the forests. Bees are aggressive in nature, and species like the Asian hornet are known for being a dominating and aggressive brood killer and feeder of its own and other bee species. Asian hornet also engages in wiping out the entire species like honey bee and their colonies, making it difficult to rear, but they are nevertheless reared for food. Bees are mainly consumed during autumn season, while consumption during spring is avoided, since pollination results into frequent allergic reaction to bee-eaters (Kay et al. 2009; Baker 2016). This allergic reaction is however common among many people, even when the bees are harvested in autumn. Despite such health ordeal, bees and bees' larvae remained as the most prized insect among this tribe. Bees are normally cooked dry or fried, with or without condiments, and it is known for its high content of

protein and amino acids.

3.3. WOOD-BORING LARVAE

Wood-Boring Larvae of the Asian long-horned beetle

or *Anoplophora glabripennis* [*Kachāt*] is also

extensively and popularly consumed by the tribe.

They are collected from live or dying (rotting) trees,

which the wood boring beetle infest and gives birth to.

Anoplophora glabripennis usually range from three

inches in length, and half to one inch in breadth

(Gordh and McKirdy 2013). There are again white

round-headed wood boring larvae, which are more

easily available than the red round-headed wood

boring larvae, which are extremely rare to get. Unlike the white species, the red ones produce strong smell, which adds to the taste. The taste of the 'round-headed borers' is similar to prawn, although it is much murkier and thicker in taste owing to high content of protein and amino acids (Gordh and McKirdy 2013; USDA 2001). Taking the emphasis of the United Nations on insects substituting meat with its high protein, these larvae may become one of the most desired insect for its high protein content.

3.4. CHINESE MYSTERY SNAIL

Heliculture is also practiced on a small scale by the tribe, although many still resorts to collecting from terrace field or from wetlands. Snails are nocturnal in nature, and hence they are collected or harvested right after the rain. Among the many types of snails found, the Chinese Mystery Snail or *Bellamya chinensis* [*khorbunglā*] is consumed extensively among the Tāngkhuls. Unlike the French serving it as starters, or appetizers, or entrée, this snail is consumed as main course food by them. Bellamya chinensis which measures around 2 ½" from foot to tail and about 1 ¼" in diameter (Oguoma and Ohajianya 2007; Kperegbeyi 2014). Taken from this context, and its globose shell with 6 to 7 whorls, the Bellamya chinensis can be considered as being the

Insects and Sustainability: The Practice of Entomophagy Among the Tāngkhul-Naga Tribe of Manipur

largest among snail types. Adult snail is normally olive greenish, or brown greenish in colour, with an operculum that forms as trap door closes the front of the snail. Snails are known for carrying parasites that causes Meningitis, therefore requiring rigorous cleaning and cooking (Kperegbeyi 2014). The common preparation and cooking the Bellamya chinensis among the Tāngkhuls involved cleaning the snail by taking out the operculum, cutting the tail with knives, boiling the snail with salt, drenching the boiled after five minutes, and later cooking with mint leaves, potatoes, or pork.

Insects and Sustainability: The Practice of Entomophagy Among the Tāngkhul-Naga Tribe of Manipur

Chinese Mystery Snail or *Bellamya chinensis*

(after taking out the Operculum)

Insects and Sustainability: The Practice of Entomophagy Among the Tāngkhul-Naga Tribe of Manipur

Snail is spongy-chewy in texture, and slimy and earthy in taste and flavour. Snails contain high protein, iron, vitamin B12, magnesium, selenium, and Omega-3, thereby helping in the building of red blood cells, maintaining the nervous system and immune system healthy, strengthening bones, and maintaining healthy heart (Kperegbeyi 2014).

3.5. GRASSHOPPER (*CATANTOPIDAE*)

Insects are no doubt known for being a food supplement, and in rural Ukhrul district, insects helped the undernourished children with minerals and vitamin content. For instance, children who suffer from deficiency of protein can get protein from

Insects and Sustainability: The Practice of Entomophagy Among the Tāngkhul-Naga Tribe of Manipur

consuming grasshoppers. Grasshoppers contain amino acids that help in curtailing kwashiorkor, which is a protein deficiency that many children in undeveloped countries suffer, causing physical and neurological impediment. Consuming grasshopper is well-known among the Tāngkhuls, and while there are as many as 23,000 types of grasshoppers in the world (Slade 2008), and among this the *Catantopidae* species [*Khāo*] are widely consumed by the Tāngkhuls. The Catantopidae grasshoppers are available in the post rice-harvest terrace fields during winter. This grasshopper is widely available in China, and given the geographical proximity of China and

North-East India, *Catantopidae* remains widely available (Chunmei and Xinyue 1998). Preparing grasshopper as main course food requires a tedious process, since all its ovipositors and legs needs to be pulled off, to disallow getting stuck in the throat. With its crunchy and nutty taste, roasted or fried grasshoppers are known to possess thrice the same amount of protein as beef, and remain rich in micronutrients like iron and zinc.

3.6. TESSARATOMIDAE (SCUTELLERIDAE)

The tribe is also found of consuming Tessaratomidae of the Scutelleridae family [*Lenghik*]. Tessaratomidae eliminates offensive juice odour when they are

Insects and Sustainability: The Practice of Entomophagy Among the Tāngkhul-Naga Tribe of Manipur

disturbed by bug hunters (Roychoudhury, Joshi, and Rawat 1994). Two types of Tessaratomidae– one found in trees and the other in the water, are consumed; and while the tree Tessaratomidae are not easily available, water amphibian Tessaratomidae are available throughout the year (Roychoudhury, Joshi, and Rawat 1994). The common consumption habit of this bug involves deep frying the bug, roasting, and mashing it together with chilies and to make *chutney*. They are also eaten raw by sucking the juice of the insects, which many children playfully indulged into.

Insects and Sustainability: The Practice of Entomophagy Among the Tāngkhul-Naga Tribe of Manipur

Tessaratomidae

Interestingly, the colour of the Tessaratomidae changes when the juice is being sucked out. The Tāngkhul tribe also extensively engaged in consuming Barklice or *Psocoptera* [*Mikzur*]. This insect is often found in gregarious form, and they run in erratic manner when they are disturbed. The insect produces strong smell that are believed to add taste to the insect (Dunn 1996). *Psocoptera* are scavengers and are found in many trees, which allows easy harvesting, and therefore does not require rearing or farming the insects (Borror and White 1998; Gibb 2014).

3.7. BARK LICE AND BLACK AND YELLOW GARDEN SPIDER
Bark lice are often consumed by roasting together with beans by the tribe. Black and Yellow Garden Spider or *Argiope aurantia* [*Karkao*] are also consumed extensively, although it is difficult to procure this insect. Found in dense forests, webbed

and nestled in the trees, picking normally involves rolling the web with twined twigs and killing the bug within the web (Robinson 2005). Yellow spiders are often found in groups, making the hunting of this insect to become easier, although it is found in dense forest. Yellow spiders are normally roasted or fried for consumption, and remains fatty and bitter in taste.

Bark Lice

Insects and Sustainability: The Practice of Entomophagy

Among the Tāngkhul-Naga Tribe of Manipur

3.6. WATER AND RAIN INSECTS

Some of the popular water insects consumed as food come in the form of Dragonfly Nymph or *Anisoptera [Simuklā]*, Water Scorpion or *Nepa Cinerea [Āwo Kasār]*, and Black and Oval Water Scavenger Beetles or *Hydrophilidae [Kongriksei]*. All these are water predators and they feed on smaller insects (Burton and Burton 2002). They are either found in the wetlands, terrace fields, and inside water bodies, and are easily captured with fishing nets or picked up. Dragonfly nymph is rather juicy and salty in taste, and has low fat content. Water Scorpion and Black and Oval Water Scavenger Beetles are somehow similar in taste and texture, and the Tāngkhuls usually chipped their wings before preparing it as dish.

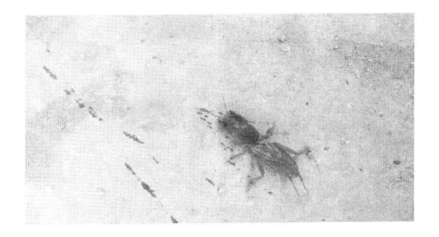

Mole Cricket or *Gryllotalpa*

Mole Cricket or *Gryllotalpa* [*Rātkha*], rather prized and belonging to the cricket family is one of the type of mole cricket consumed by the tribe. Mole cricket is specially found in wetlands, making the terrace fields to be their main habitat (Pessarakli 2008). Although

Insects and Sustainability: The Practice of Entomophagy Among the Tāngkhul-Naga Tribe of Manipur

farmers consider them as pest, the insect constitute one of the main course dishes for the tribe, and they serve the squishy, nutty, and fatty insect with traditional herbs and red chillies. Consumed during the rainy season, Termites Swarmers (Asian Alates) or *Isoptera* [*Malum*] also served as food for the tribe (Jackman and Drees 1998).

Insects and Sustainability: The Practice of Entomophagy Among the Tāngkhul-Naga Tribe of Manipur

Termite Swarmers or *Asian alates*

Photo Credit: Kachuiwung Ronra Shimray

Termites offer an excellent food choice when they are being roasted. Termites are known for containing high protein and carbohydrate, giving people the capacity to maintain balanced diet. Termite Swarmers come out from their hive during the rainy season (May/June), and the tribe catches the insect from their hive or when they fly out. While roasting, the wings get easily removed, and the remains are fried with spices and eaten with main course meal. Termite swarmers are also used as "traps" to catch birds.

Insects and Sustainability: The Practice of Entomophagy

Among the Tāngkhul-Naga Tribe of Manipur

Insects and Sustainability: The Practice of Entomophagy Among the Tāngkhul-Naga Tribe of Manipur

CHAPTER III: DISCUSSION AND CONCLUSION

In terms of thinking 'progressive food development', insects provide with an option to come up with different food alternatives. The tribe can take initiative in rearing and harvesting insects to improve the livelihood of the people. However, since farming and rearing insects is not practiced on a wide scale, most edible insects are gathered in the forests seasonally, and have come to constitute a luxury item to serve some niche markets of the Tāngkhuls, like the 'Womens' Market Phungreitang Colony'. Preserving insects are also not technically feasible owing to innovative and financial challenges at present. That

Insects and Sustainability: The Practice of Entomophagy Among the Tāngkhul-Naga Tribe of Manipur

being said, entomophagy can be encouraged on wide scale in the line of sustainability practices among this tribe, since control over protein through consumption of insects will have more advantage over sustainable food in the future. In short, the tribal poor in rural region with their chronic food shortage can look towards alternative food practices, and organized insect farming on a larger scale, when such awareness is imparted, and technologically becomes feasible.

Food is a determinant of building the structure of societies, thereby playing fundamental role in economy and culture. The economic and cultural food

Insects and Sustainability: The Practice of Entomophagy Among the Tāngkhul-Naga Tribe of Manipur

consumption pattern of any society or community is again conditioned by environment and geo-structure that surrounds them, although globalization is breaking down such barriers through homogenization and standardization of products. Amidst such changes is the ability of the entomophagy to influence one's own communities and beyond in modern days, and the insectivorous diet of the Tāngkhuls can work towards such cross-cultural and trans-national influence. Sutton (1990) shows that there is a growth of spontaneous cultural evolution as well as scarcity of meat in the fast moving globalized world, and this may lead anthropo-entomophagy to become a

Insects and Sustainability: The Practice of Entomophagy Among the Tāngkhul-Naga Tribe of Manipur

common gourmet culture across the world. Research from Huis shows that compared to other cattle and pigs being reared, insects reared for consumption produces significantly lower quantities of greenhouse gases, thereby proving that insects are environmentally friendlier, with higher protein. In terms of environment and in terms of solving food crisis, people should therefore look towards entomophagy as the main alternatives to animals. Insects can easily fulfill the food security requirements with less environmental impact, and supplement human diet with high protein, minerals, vitamins, some fats, and carbohydrates for the perfect balanced diet.

REFERENCES

Aruga, Hisao. 1994. *Principles of Sericulture*. London: A.A. Balkema.

Baker, Kevin. 2016. *The World's Most Dangerous Animals*. New York: eBookIt.com.

Bodenheimer, F. S. 2013. *Insects as Human Food : A Chapter of the Ecology of Man*. Dordrecht.

Borror, Donald J. (Donald Joyce), and Richard E. White. 1998. *A Field Guide to Insects: America North of Mexico*. Boston: Houghton Mifflin

Insects and Sustainability: The Practice of Entomophagy Among the Tāngkhul-Naga Tribe of Manipur

Harcourt.

Burton, Maurice, and Robert Burton. 2002. *International Wildlife Encyclopedia*. New York: Marshall Cavendish.

Chunmei, Huang, and Cheng Xinyue. 1998. "The Fauna of Catantopidae and Its Origin in China and Adjacent Region." *Kun Chong Xue Bao. Acta Entomologica Sinica* 42 (2): 184–98.

Defoliart, Gene R. 1999. "Insecs as Food: Why the Western Attitude Is Important." *Annu. Rev. Entomol* 44 (80): 21–50. doi:10.1146/annurev.ento.44.1.21.

Insects and Sustainability: The Practice of Entomophagy

Among the Tāngkhul-Naga Tribe of Manipur

Dunn, Gary A. 1996. *Insects of the Great Lakes Region*. Ann Arbor: University of Michigan Press.

FAO. 2013. *Edible Insects. Future Prospects for Food and Feed Security. Food and Agriculture Organization of the United Nations*. Vol. 171. doi:10.1017/CBO9781107415324.004.

Gibb, Timothy. 2014. *Contemporary Insect Diagnostics: The Art and Science of Practical Entomology*. New York: Academic Press.

Goldman, Phyllis Barkas. 1992. *Monkeyshines Goes Buggy: The Study of Entomology*. Greensboro: EBSCO Publishing, Inc.

Insects and Sustainability: The Practice of Entomophagy Among the Tāngkhul-Naga Tribe of Manipur

Gordh, Gordon, and Simon McKirdy. 2013. *The Handbook of Plant Biosecurity: Principles and Practices for the Identification, Containment and Control of Organisms That Threaten Agriculture and the Environment Globally.* New York: Springer Science & Business Media.

Holt, Vincent M. 1885. *Why Not Eat Insects?* London: Leadenhall Press.

Jackman, John A., and Bastiaan M. Drees. 1998. *A Field Guide to Common Texas Insects.* Taylor Trade Publishing.

Kay, A. Barry, Jean Bousquet, Patrick G. Holt, and

Allen P. Kaplan. 2009. *Allergy and Allergic Diseases*. London: Blackwell Publishing.

Kperegbeyi, J.I. 2014. "A Survey Of Backyard (Small-Scale) Heliculture System in Delta State, Nigeria." *Journal of Environmental Sciences and Policy Evaluation* 4 (1): 24–31.

Narasaiah, M. Lakshmi. 2003. *Problems and Prospects of Sericulture*. New Delhi: Discovery Pub. House.

Oguoma, N. N., and D. O. Ohajianya. 2007. "Potentials in Financing Heliculture under the Agricultural Credit Guarantee Scheme in Imo and

Rivers' States of Nigeria: A Comparative Analysis." *International Journal of Agriculture and Rural Development* 9 (1). School of Agriculture and Agricultural Technology, Federal University of Technology: 48–54. doi:10.4314/ijard.v9i1.2665.

Pager, H. 1973. "Rock Paintings in Southern Africa Showing Bees and Honey Hunting." *Bee World* 54 (2). Taylor & Francis: 61–68. doi:10.1080/0005772X.1973.11097456.

Pessarakli, Mohammad. 2008. *Handbook of Turfgrass Management and Physiology*. London: CRC Press.

Insects and Sustainability: The Practice of Entomophagy

Among the Tāngkhul-Naga Tribe of Manipur

Ramos-Elorduy, Julieta. 2009. "Anthropo-Entomophagy: Cultures, Evolution and Sustainability." *Entomological Research* 39 (5). Blackwell Publishing Asia: 271–88. doi:10.1111/j.1748-5967.2009.00238.x.

Robinson, William H. 2005. *Urban Insects and Arachnids: A Handbook of Urban Entomology*. Cambridge: Cambridge University Press.

Roychoudhury, N., K. C. Joshi, and P. S. Rawat. 1994. "A New Record of TessaratomidaePurpureus Westwood (Heteroptera Scutelleridae) on Poplar, Populus Deltoides Bartr. Ex Marsh." *Indian Forester* 120

Insects and Sustainability: The Practice of Entomophagy Among the Tāngkhul-Naga Tribe of Manipur

(12): 1126–28.

Slade, Suzanne. 2008. *Grasshoppers*. New York: PowerKids Press.

Spiegel, Majolein van der. 2015. "Safety of Food Based on Insects." In *Regulating Safety of Traditional and Ethnic Foods*, edited by V. (Vishweshwaraiah) Prakash, Olga Martín-Belloso, Larry Keener, S. (Siân) Astley, Susanne Braun, Helena McMahon, and Huub Lelieveld. Oxford: Academic Press.

Sutton, M. 1990. "Insecsts Resources and Pliopleistocene Hominid Evolution." In

Insects and Sustainability: The Practice of Entomophagy Among the Tāngkhul-Naga Tribe of Manipur

Ethnobiology: Implications and Applications, edited by Darrell Addison Posey, 197–205. Belem: Museu Paraense Emilio Goeldi.

Tan, Hui Shan Grace, Arnout R.H. Fischer, Patcharaporn Tinchan, Markus Stieger, L.P.A. Steenbekkers, and Hans C.M. van Trijp. 2015. "Insects as Food: Exploring Cultural Exposure and Individual Experience as Determinants of Acceptance." *Food Quality and Preference* 42 (June): 78–89. doi:10.1016/j.foodqual.2015.01.013.

USDA. 2001. *Wanted, the Asian Longhorned Beetle - United States. Animal and Plant Health*

Insects and Sustainability: The Practice of Entomophagy Among the Tāngkhul-Naga Tribe of Manipur

Inspection Service. Washington: U.S. Dept. of Agriculture, Animal and Plant Health Inspection Service.

van Huis, Arnold, Dennis G. A. B. Oonincx, Joost van Itterbeeck, Marcel J. W. Heetkamp, Henry van den Brand, and Joop J. A. van Loon. 2010. "An Exploration on Greenhouse Gas and Ammonia Production by Insect Species Suitable for Animal or Human Consumption." Edited by Immo A. Hansen. *PLoS ONE* 5 (12). Public Library of Science: e14445. doi:10.1371/journal.pone.0014445.

Printed in Great Britain
by Amazon